# A

# PRESENCE

# OF

# ANGELS

Judyth Hill

SHERMAN
SA SHER
Publishing

Grateful acknowledgment is given for the permission to reprint the following poems from previous collections:

From *The Goddess Cafe*, Fish Drum, Santa Fe, NM: *Joan of Arc, Give Me Back My Innocence, A Moon Can Look at a Poet*

From *Hardwired for Love*, Pennywhistle Press, Santa Fe, NM: *When the Men Get It, We're All In Luck Men and Angelfood, The House That Jack Built, Samurai Angels, That's Good, That's Enough* (Title is from a line in *Two Birds Walking* by Tess Gallagher)

From *New Mexico Poetry Renaissance*, Red Crane Books, Santa Fe, NM: *(A Dream of Frida) Samurai Angels, Grist for Grace*

From *Saludos, Poems of New Mexico*, Pennywhistle Press, Santa Fe, NM: *Don't Show This to Anyone*


Collection edited by Nancy Fay and Judith Asher
Cover Art by New Grub Street Design, Santa Fe, New Mexico
Cover photograph of Judyth Hill by Bob Wartell
Printed in the USA by Marrakech Express, Tarpon Springs, Florida
Type set in Matrix Book from Emigre Fonts on acid free paper

First Edition
ISBN 0-9644196-1-0


All inquiries and permission requests should be addressed to the Publisher

Sherman Asher Publishing
P.O. Box 2853
Santa Fe, NM, 87504
505-984-2686

*For My Angels:*

*Cassidy amd Amanda Jane Hill*
*and heart of my heart, John Townley*

# A PRESENCE OF ANGELS

## COIN OF THE REALM

How valuable to tremble,
in your presence,
a shudder of vowels,
praising the white shoulders of sleep.
Light swallows sleep and roosters.
I listen for your mysterious breath,
tunneling lonely towards morning,
dreaming of columbines,
guitarrons, and citronella.
In night's tender moss,
the smell of roses is an arrow on fire.
We take aim and find first light like cool milk.
Drink to a day of stringed instruments.
We take the open road. Count off twenty centuries.
I am afraid of nothing, but with my body of skin and music
awake.

# ANOTHER SEASON WITH ANGELS

I am where Picasso left his last masterpiece in lichen.
It's the forest museum.
Butter scented Ponderosas guard the wild strawberry,
beg us, please touch,
come closer,
please taste.

We enroll in the Berlitz of the woods, and become fluent.
We stop our searching for answers,
and find the barrel cactus in secret, vivid bloom.
We stop our longing to be good,
and find an overhang that will be good to us
when July storms hurtle in.

Because I didn't learn you, I met you.
And I didn't study you, I stayed with you.
Because I stopped trying, my beauty found me.
I stopped writing, and the rivers and bosques
began to write me.

## ANGELS AND THORNS

The first part is about angels.
Wings. Lots of air...
You know how that is. Or do you?
Then there's the thorns.
We know that. The piercing.
The erotic edge.
The touch of harm.
Then that flutter.
Air and rescue,
Wind and the swift descent.
But Jacob, Jacob saw them on the ladder.
And remember, they were going up and coming down.
He knew to build the Temple there.
Because that's where it was.

# FOURTEEN SNAPSHOTS OF ANGEL

Synopsis:
Your back is to the camera.
This film stars Charlie Chaplin and the angels.
Each angel has a speaking part, but you are silent.
Each angel flies around snowy treetops.
The white drifts beneath show a shadow you can hardly bear.
It sizzles off the cold screen.
Suddenly, it's so light,
you tell your story to anyone that will listen.

\*\*\*

Angels are like department store fashion.
They come in a size that almost fits.
You look good in red, but they are out of that color.
You consider changing the buttons.
You take them to the dressing room. You try and try.
At home, your bed is strewn with angels.
Cast off angels, angels with torn hems, held by safety pins.
You borrow angels from your friends.
If you open your closet, wings are beating,
you can hardly hear.
You want to wear them all.
You realize what it might mean to be human.

\*\*\*

In their marionette life,
angels dance on strings.
Their arms lift and fall.
It's not despair, but it looks that way.

Backstage, there is a tangle of thin strands,
thin strands like silk,
just like silk.

\*\*\*

I've fallen in love with angels.
I do my hair the way they like.
I wear amethysts. I put gold coins in my mouth.
I call them daily.
Hello, I say. Darling, I call them.
My darling. I imagine clouds and blow kisses.
I talk so quickly, they almost notice me.
This is called prayer.

\*\*\*

Linguistical Note:
Angel is Tewa for God.

Historical Note:
Headline in local newspaper reads,
Two angels shot while escaping from the newly fenced
School for Boys in Springer, New Mexico.

\*\*\*

Mozart saw angels.
When he wrote the Requiem, cruel black wings
fluttered around his head.
And the bag of gold coins.
See, there it is again.
Sharps, flats and feathers. A minor key of flight.
A whir, a swirl of chords. In the distance,
very faint, the angels going
make a sound like roses.

My mother forbids me to write anything awful.
I must love angels.
I must love her.
I am good and must prove it.
There can't be knives or pills or sealed train cars
in this or any other poem.
She will check.
The angels will leave.

\*\*\*

Boddhisattva had lunch with the angels.
Under his tree they ate pasta salad, pasta primavera,
tricolor rigatoni. Always Italian.
Lots of bread dipped in calamata olive oil,
generous grinds of pepper.
They chanted angel mantras and drank chianti.
They rubbed his sweet, sweet belly and ate gelato with tiny spoons.
Swords swirled overhead. They swallowed thin mints &
Buddha laughed at nothing in particular.

\*\*\*

The angels in Eden were hovering in the Tree.
They were waiting for the future to catch up to them.
Later, Daniel saw them and thought they were lions.
They wrote in Angel graffiti:
A great miracle happened/will happen/is happening here.

\*\*\*

Angel Facts:
Angel x Angel = insight.

Light is neither wave nor particle to angels
but something we can't name.
They think in the absence of gravity.
$Angel^2$ = laughter.
When we make love, angels multiply.
You can't subtract angels from anything.
Fractions don't appear in the same thought as angels.

•••

Once upon a time, you found the Beloved too hot, too cold,
or just right.
You were granted three wishes.
You could choose from a ring of ivory, gold or onyx.
You helped the ants, freed the raven and fed the bear.
If a coach were to pass by right now,
that same silver key would rattle in your pocket.
What this has to do with angels, only you know.

•••

Open your booklet to page one.
Journeys are to forests,
as angels are to blank.
Windows are to
Times up. Put your pencil down.
Start singing.

•••

The angels hold in air.
Then you whirl up.
Everything in your own autumn is turning at once.
Leaves fall. Whatever is white is still as glass.
Transparent. Everything on screen goes black.
You see through to angel.

# WHEN THE MEN GET IT, WE'RE ALL IN LUCK

When Rumi saw the house, he knew the Beloved lived there.
Palace Avenue it's not, more like 12th field to your right,
turn south at the patch of bluebells.
It was the Beloved's house, and the poet gathered the men there.
They complained about the dishes and the lack of facilities.
They took care of the children and did all the cooking.
It was a grove of men.
They kept thinking, we should fix up this old house.
But the poet said No! God is a radish! Get it?
Let the house be and play with the children!
Forget the plumbing and eat all the peaches!
Don't rebuild the carburetor, make wild music!
Then eat.
Then eat again, then sleep.
Let's get all mixed up, the poet says.
Let's call the yellow flowers by another name.
Let's make lists of fruits and hang them from the axes.
Let's use all the plates, then forget meal times.
Go right to kneeling, straight to praying.
Let's spin like dervishes.
Let's throw dice for who cooks and who cleans and then let's cheat.
Let's have only fun.
Let's let the women back,
tell them we've got it, and it's about
radishes!

## MEN AND ANGELFOOD

Men love angelfood because they wish women were like that.
Light and sweet, sweet as a kind of dessert
that melts on the tongue,
because the air in it is trapped by the stiffness of beat and heat.
It's sweet, angelfood, and fluffy.
It bears no grudges, holds no weight,
doesn't argue and may even do windows.
Is maybe a window in cake form,
a view of men's longing for our softness,
our delicate melting on their tongues,
but gluey too,
sticky to their hearts and fingers.
Remember the odd serving piece that is only an angelfood cutter?
A cake that has summoned its own utensil
is a man's kind of cake.
Think of the tender prongs, stroke them,
theirs is the music of after dinner.
Dishes cleared and this light, floating effort at sweetness
brought on china and accompanied by its own tool
and men will tell you when you ask,
Angelfood is my favorite.
And in this we can also see
how they long to offer their own trapped sweetness
late in the evening, to us.

ABSINTHE MAKES THE ART GROW

He looked into the center of the sunflower.
The world whirred, roared.
All the way yellow too loud,
unbearable, a siren of petals.
A swelter of, a startle of

Clotted green, seed-bearing
A crop of color.

He was beaten on an anvil of wind.
The Mistral, blowing a bruise against his mind.
Anyone would have gone under in this wave.

That murder of crows.
His brother, on his knees
in the gallery,
paintings stacked from floor to ceiling.

A howling of
a herd of
a pod of
a predicament of paintings
a presence of angels

The light going on in a blare,
a disaster,
a mine collapsing inward.
Cypress swirling upwards.
His genius rising back to God like incense.

Smoke signals spelling
hurt me hurt me hurt me

Paint me a copse of
         a grove of
a pride of,
a gaggle of geese, an agony of iris.

Let all the others be forever a tribe,
12 of the Jews
11 of the Sufis
Leave Vincent alone.

It's not imaginary.
He painted what was there.
Don't you see the trees writhe,
An alarm of stars?

He wrote to Theo,
one two buckle my

There are facts:
They had been children.
He had been a minister.
He ate tomatoes, Camembert,
fresh basil, with Gauguin.

He cut his, but you know that.

Let it end this time with Theo,
in a gallery filled with white noise,
the swift winged ascent.

The silence is deafening.

II

# JACKSON POLLACK DISCOVERS ZENO'S ARROW

Paint flew:
blue twisting a thread in air, braiding
into azul, and before it lands,
Rimsky-Korsakov lets out a sigh.
Expressionism is born in a tea-cup.
The leaves are read.
The mystic tells the artist:
      Supreme good fortune without blame
      It furthers one to cross the Great Waters.
But the artist says,
      I can't travel anymore.
      Ever since Picasso invented Cubism,
      I can only get as far as the corner.
Then sleek skinned ropes of red rivered
into Maypole, into June, July
and the stationary whirr of hummingbird, 100 beats per second.

You could hear lilacs open, and faintly,
the crush of irises unfold,
the scent of bread rising.
Wisteria rings white like tiny bells.
Absolutely Japanese, the black, black pulse and dot,
a crisis of crimson, a pool of blue cooling,
but before, in air,
the colors, they hold there,
form and unform, shapeshift,
a Torah of light.
Streams of color spell the Holy Name,
a tehillim of praise. Hosannah,
the Angels sing in fourpart dissonant harmony, D natural.
We smell The Russian Revolution, the fall of China,
and the colors have almost reached the canvas,
an epiphany.

At that moment, Newton wakes, screaming,
I was wrong, I was wrong, and Einstein laughs,
I told you, I told you! Garbo says nothing.

Daffodils and crocuses bloom across hillsides.
Rivers, worldround, run one millimoment faster,
making just that much more splash
joining hydrogen to oxygen in an ecstacy of plenty.
The galaxy widens, actually widens by ten syllables
and the wingspan of an oriole.
Rimbaud instantly regrets his lost poems,
I should have kept writing, he cries.
But he'd seen inside the witch's cave.
Now it's time for us to go there, and fling
vowels into the darkness.

Say A, the creamy sigh of lovers, E, the exit into light and never,
I and I and U get the point.

It's post-modern. Time tossing gold tokens into the meter,
taking the crosstown bus to the infinite.
Asking the Crone, Isn't this my stop?
And the colors, they're only inches and centuries away.
Civilizations fall and we say the word,
the secret, single sound that ignites letters into black stars.

In a breath, a heartbeat,
the paint lands on Pollack's canvas,
in simple, chaotic accord.

(A DREAM OF FRIDA)


Vines grow up, around the coverlet
where the artist sleeps.
A ghost of hyacinths floats above her
wired to explode into a destiny of calamity.

She dreams herself into her future, where vines grow
around a wisteria trellis and she's walking,
walking the Hacienda's veranda, and vine's entwine
flower to needle, leaf to bud, to bloom, seed
and leaves again, then dry, they fall,
fall and blow.

Easterly wind, October's heat takes the bosque down into golden,
vines grow up, around a skeleton month
where no mother calls the name of her daughter,
no one strokes her head, calls her, mi corazon, mi caratida.

She's alone by the Rio, a glint of light
shiny coins of water music clinking,
moving swift over rocks, where vines grow up
in the sleep of aspens.
They quiet, calm them, as horses do. by breath.
A tree breathes into autumn:
A woman sleeps under a yellow quilt of leaves.

Grasses lay down, apples are sudden
in an orchard of over.

November calls her by name.
Something she can't see, strokes her again.
Her mother becomes visible on the stairs of the Hacienda.
Her mother is singing on the veranda,

a girlhood song in perfect Castilian.
No tiene miedo, she sings.
She sings of shadow and light, sombre y luz.
She strokes the bannister as she descends.
She walks the long road to the river,
the cottonwoods arch overhead.
Moonlight peers through bare branches and clouds.

She sees color. The night is a new dress.
She carries a bouquet of bones to the edge of the water.
Vines grow up around the fallen poplars,
she never catches her breath.
She runs from the voice calling her name.
The road is stuttering in tree.
The trees sing in Spanish of falling.

The yellow quilt is spread under a wisteria vine
in full fragrant bloom.
Her hair is tied back with a lilac ribbon.
Her mother wears a dress of shadow.
She is drowning in a bed of white bones.

She hasn't worn lace in years.
Her day is set to go off on a hairpin trigger.

Anything can make her go down that road.
She saw it once, quickly around a corner in the Museum.
She's walking, walking up the stairs dressed in fallen leaves.
It was a landscape painted in 1806.
It was the French countryside, but exactly the same.
That gold, the bones, the leaves in drift.

She never knew the painter's name.
She called it once in a dream.
He came to her dressed in velvet.

He lay in the dark bed, whispering
Sombre, sombre, te amo.
She whispered back.

There was no map to this place.
The Museum was in Milan.
The dream was tangled in her hair.
The vines grew up the trellis to the second floor.
She slept on as if nothing had happened.

# THE REST OF LORCA'S BALLAD

I can't listen to you, white,
slicing clouds across the gypsy moon.
She just laughs, and returns as icicle
to all the daughters
turning delicate pirouettes, the wind their partner.

I can't marry you, violet,
Shadows of bees weave through the branches of the olive.
It must be night, because the taste of sweet mint
is suddenly bitter.

I won't travel with you, green,
with your sash of sorrow,
your chambray wedding shirt,
your hoarfrost over the ground
too soon in August.

Muchacha, muchacha, says the black railing
around the seawalk.
I can't repeat what the sailor said,
that morning we were so intimate under early stars.
On the plaza
all the women stared.
Let them, I said.
No me olvides, I said.

We looked into the cistern.
Small frogs chirped the day awake.
We wrapt our arms about each other's waist,
and promised many things, saddles
mirrors and doves.

It no longer matters, red.
100 brown roses would change nothing.
Orange, like yellow,
is ignorant of this story.

From the balcony, her cool voice beckoned,
a slip of a girl, young, broken,
forgotten by blue.

## DUCHAMP'S GAMBIT

The constraints of density wore him down.
Not less, the considerations of space, time.
What is the question if the answer is art?

Queen to queen's pawn, he thought.
At least the pieces move.

Everything had gotten too complicated at last,
each shard, shred of paper, tatters of thoughts
broken into the smallest possible glimpse
where something had happened.

Nothing became possible.

When the nude descended the staircase, it was, you need
to understand, final: how time broke delicately apart and fanned
out, until the only possible
way to understand anything,
one's life, art, the simple downward
descent of the utterly human,
is to hold the moment as fragment
except, the motion slows, until;
each gesture is finite and distracted from any whole.

Life becomes nonsensical. Reality becomes particle.
We need that wave, that way for gesture to collapse
on itself into meaning.
Pawn to king's rook.
Each move is a whole, but is it relief enough?
He couldn't believe in painting any further.
He was off the board, past the sanctity of squared space.
The world needed to catch up.  He waited,
ready with any number of moves in a checkered mind gone black on white.

he will never reach the bottom tread,
never step down onto

Everything, one supposes, simply got too heavy.
Density of minutia overwhelmed him.
Even
Glass, sinks, paint, the mundane had betrayed him.
The ready made was already perfected, why make?

Nothing was simple enough to express on one canvas,
let alone one lifetime.
Finally even dust, that patient residue of the delusion of clock time,
turned out to be important.
It was unbearable, the sheer weight of it all,
a chocolate grinder, a musical note, the Greek word for salt.
Let alone color.
Imagine the oppressive potential in the vibratory rate of green.

You could only pray never to understand this.
You know he had to know.
If he thought about it, he could barely shave, or eat.
A fork lifted to the mouth in a future of forevers.

Chess was the only sane response.
Each move, closer to an ending, and the
king, lonely, stripped bare of wife, home defenders,
even god, standing stock still, at rest,
this might be a kind of victory. Not like

his own next thought,
His final piece was made in secret.

## SEEN AS ANGEL

> "If it were not for the anxiety behind those apples,
> Cezanne would not interest me
> any more than Bouguereau."
>
> Pablo Picasso

The problem is perspective,
Where do you stand?

Color hounded him, hurt him into apples.
No life is still,
but apples, biscuits, a jug,
merely caught becoming
color and mass.

Light slows, distilled from wave into particle.
Can you slow down your looking until you see purely
color and mass?
Until it's so heavy, it can hold in air.
Until, it's light.

Any landscape seen slow enough is abstract.

It's not perspective.
It doesn't matter where you set the easel.

Mont Sainte-Victoire should have been a safe bet.
A painter should be able to see a moutain.
It's not going anywhere,

but Cezanne knew
his looking was breaking the world apart, each patch and
thin
stitch of paint.

He could not allow us to see the figure and landscape as any more
real than the way the colors

This is not a finished report.
This is the primacy of question, of
Dislocation.
In a dilated stillpoint, all the tenses
converge, present past future

What could that be but
abstract?
He worried.
That sentence hadn't been said yet, wouldn't be, for years.

Do apples really fall, he wondered?
Is flesh really red?
It
was a question, broken into cones and spheres.

Who wouldn't be anxious?
Time slowed, and he
moving faster than the whole generation,
stopped color.
Light on its way to red, is green.
Cezanne, in his hurry to invent the future, took it as it was,

Leda's flesh is green.
When you see an apple it all makes sense.

I have not the richness of color, he complained.
Nothing was good enough,
gravity failed, and apples,
perched impossibly on the broken plane of the table,

held.
Still he worried.
Every brushstroke ended with a question,
 a what if offered against all other choices.
How much light does it take to screw in a shadow?

Light became increasingly diffuse. He answered his question
by abolishing the obvious.

Who cares what time it is,
if time is not linear, and space is not empty.
Apples and mountains, bathers in a sensation of light.

A static light
Space is not empty,
it's singing.

Leaving space on the canvas to prove it.

The landscape dislocates,
time compresses.
Perhaps, he thought,
there is no best place to stand.

On the table, the basket, pear or skull,
the ginger jar,
each seen
from a separate angle of vision.
It's the entire world in a blink.

This is how fast angels move to hold still.
This is what they see.

Color became the perspective:
warm advances, cool recedes.
It's a map of reality.
The text was apples.

A primer of apples.
A is for red
yellow blue. It's primary.
He tore his hair out, yelled at his friends,
slunk from his mistress.
He worked. A tedium, a torment.

They say he painted more
apples
than he could ever have eaten in a lifetime.
Who was counting?
The apple perched at any angle, won't roll.

This isn't Newton's universe anymore,
it's a free for all.
Anything goes. Anything stays.
No straight lines in this world, I promise you.

Who was measuring?

The anxiety behind the apples.
Today you will be tested on apples.
Aren't they easy?
Aren't they still real?
Maybe not real anymore, but aren't they still?
If we put them with biscuits on a tilted table are they still
quiet?
Are they a life?

A is for
He made the alphabet of modern.
He's the mountain every painter has to learn to see.
It doesn't matter where you stand to look.
Can you stand to look?

Paint, he said, as if you held, not saw.
He was thinking of apples,
their heft in his hand.
And the legs of Leda, that green on its way to your next glance.
Look at an apple, it makes perfect sense.

A is for the way he looked at card dealers, saw
a still life.
A is for what we can't know until we do it.
A is for art, it's simple,
just
resist the imperious pull of gravity. Resist what you know,
Resist
a flat surface making its stretch palatable to apples.

Read light as volume, read light as mass, read light as density,
Read light as matter.
The text is apples.

When he died,
he knew he was the greatest painter that had ever lived.
It worried him.

# TURNING TO GRACE

To the Galleria Uffizi our guide leads us,
  after pasta and antipasto, seven kinds
  of olives, cheeses draped with fatted meats.
  A feast Americans save for holidays
  in Florence is three times daily.
Sugo di Pomodoro agli Aromi, Minestra di pane,
Insalata con Granchi e Patate: each course a masterwork
we can't refuse and don't want.
We are eternal guests in sturdy shoes, exhausted from plenty,
the red cheeked enthusiasm of aproned women
waving platters and pictures of bambini.
Straw swaddled chianti,
we are on a bender of art, God and linguini.

Marinara and now,
the riches of four centuries splayed
in stunning confusion, a profusion of Madonnas
by Giotto and Cimabue, Raphael and Da Vinci.
The images served and re-served,
monumental and catholic.
Mother and child, gilt or gilded, a glut
of one story told over.

I rest on a velvet bench before Leonardo's
L'Annunciazione.
My attention caught by the angel,
bearing lilies and news, a plain thing, common as potatoes.
A winged man in a world of topiary,
edge of building laid in uniform and perfect corner.
And Mary, a mere girl really, at her needlework
or some busyness of the hands,
is turned, just slightly to face us,
her hand raised as if it might be possible

to turn away the grace, the grief, the child.
As if she was, just at that moment, choosing.
Her palm cupped as a womb, the gesture of vessel.
She's calm, as if she had always known
what she would bear.

I lack a reference for the look in her eyes.

Then, whatever in me that has said no for a hundred years,
that obdurate, chill and chiseled piece,
breaks in me gently.
Thin glass of grief, the slate of refusal
that keeps me stranger to my own children,
shatter
and find me willing.

# JOAN OF ARC

Why is this woman like Joan of Arc?

1. She has been on fire 500 years.
2. She's left everything behind so many times.
3. Her clothes are always wrong.
4. She hears Voices, sees Angels, and she takes their advice.
5. She's confused about sex.
6. She has to save France.

## GIVE ME BACK MY INNOCENCE

I'm your Eve, your Havah,
I'm your trouble coming to get you.
I'm that bite between your teeth,
that flesh giving way straight to juice.
My Darling, I'm the knowledge you've been looking for,
just beneath the skin,
and I break open under that sweet pressure to such tartness.
You could make a whole harvest of me today.
And I'm for you in bushels and hectares,
red bound baskets of this wet, plenty and tang on your tongue.
Bite me and know.
It's not about good and bad this time.
It's about juice and enough
and your teeth and my skin
and Fall turning on hillsides
and full fruit falling into our hands
and no one had to talk me into this!

# ALEPH - BET

A

isn't for apple. It's too used up. A is for aleph. The spirit,
the breath, all that's really there.
A is secretly for mother, apple mother, Eve.
See there's a hint - the apple in the story of the mothers.
A is for snakes,
that's in the story and promises
and didn't that snake say,

Eat This And You'll Know Everything?

What kind of woman was Eve if she didn't know everything already?
Eden was a pretty small town,
she should have known everyone's business in a blink.
Didn't she and Adam talk?
Over dinner she could have said, Honey, What did you name that whatsis?
   With the long grey thing thing up front, you know, the thing it raises
   to trumpet over to the other valley, the one with the Shadow. I bet
   with a couple of those in one day you could plow a whole acre. They
   look as strong as an...
Adam, like all men, he'd probably take a bite of his lightly sun-warmed
manna with pomegranate fraiche
and give her that blank, mystified look.
He'd say slowly, I haven't the faintest idea what you mean.
Like they had so many grey wrinkled beasties with 3 foot ears, tiny
comical tails and that nose.
Didn't he understand plain, well, whatever it was they spoke?
Anyway Adam wasn't working for a living yet.
Why do you think they call it husbandry?
He didn't need Agriculture. Just A words.
   Awesome, Audacious.
Words you used to talk to God, you know, Praise.
Stuff he likes to hear.
Great world God, Amazing. And in just 7 days.
Imagine what you could have done if you had taken your time?
Now that's a mother talking.

29

## MOTHER MAY I

Catch as catch can mirror,
Cat got your tongue mirror.
Mirror, mirror on the door,
holding open an infinity of mothers.
One mother loves me,

One mother fears me.
One mother I can't keep alive.
Another mother, a blonde one,
a good one, a kind one,
not the one whose mouth is a crimson, Revlon slash.

Count to mother.
Would you like one mother or two in your tea?
Mother + mirror = daughter.

First there is a mirror,
then there is no mother,
then there is.

A mother for your thoughts.
Knit 1, mirror 2.
A tisket, a tasket,
a green and yellow mother.

Break a mirror,
it's seven years of bad mother.
I open my jewelry box, and the pink ballerina dances in front of the red
velvet mother.

Jack and Jill went up the hill,
Jack fell down and broke his mother's heart,
and Jill became his mirror.

Everything in the mother
is closer than it appears.

Jack and Jill went up the hill,
Jack fell down and broke his mirror,
and Jill became his mother.

# A WOMAN BUILT LIKE BRICK

Driving, I saw a rock shaped just like a barn owl.
How I've come to know one owl from another is my own story.
Building a house is a secret.
None of the men my mother married
ever did it where I could see them.

It's a hermetic science still,
the sealing in, I mean.
Windows, walls,
or how a floor can support anything of weight.

There's a secret as well,
how I grew this way up.

Similar, the simple alembic:
the closing in, four walls,
thresholds of entry
and the mystery of floors.

How nothing seemed to fall through,
or if it did, I didn't notice.
A childhood anyone would mistake for shelter.

# THE HOUSE THAT JACK BUILT

This is the house that Jack built.
This is the body of the daughter
that lives in the house that Jack built.
And the mother.
See how she glowers when she sees the body of the daughter
that lives in the house that Jack built.
The father has touched the body of the daughter,
and the mother is on fire.
This is the house the fire built.

This is the voice of the daughter
that lived in the house that Jack built.
These are the words that live in the mouth of the daughter
that grew in the fire, set by the mother,
that lived in the house that Jack built.
These are the breasts that budded and grew
that should not have been touched
by the father that lived in the house with the mother on fire
that Jack built.
Here is the way that the daughter says No, and leaves the fires
that roar in the house that Jack built.
And here are the ashes she rubbed on her face
so that you'd never know, that she was the girl that grew in the house
where the fires were set and the lines were drawn and the claims were
staked to the body of the daughter
that lived in the house that Jack built.
And here are her shoes, slender and worn,
and the suitcase all packed
and the mother on fire
and the daughter in tears,
And the voice of the daughter coming out of those walls,
And the bricks come a'crumbling as she finally speaks.
And the words are the ones that say the truth,
The terrible truth
of life in the house that Jack built.

## IT'S NOT FAIR

The cows jumped over the, over the lightening rod, he'd touched it,
it was an accident, and ride a cock
ride a cock, crowing in the night, it was sirens,
it was ambulance, orange,
blue red blue red blue red light,
stop,
white line across the monitor.
It was stopped.

Fourth of July, we drive by the farm house,
the flag was at half mast, there were so many cars,
and I wondered, a party?
All the women bringing covered dishes, pies,
the men taking their hats off in the driveway.

He was twenty-three, out on a summer job,
he was holding an irrigation pipe,
it touched the utility wire.

A month later, my daughter Amanda,
driving by says,
Mommy, are they still crying?

All week, that autumn, cows bellowed and hollered in the meadow.
I ask my neighbor, is it the full moon, or a bull come round?
No, he tells me,
They've sold the yearlings off, that's the mothers.

The winter birds start to come in, the Stellar jays
with their antics, their click and chirp,
their fearless wheeling in, all cluck and harrow.
Nuthatches run up and down the trunks of the Ponderosa,
the skittish junkos swing tree to tree.

It's raucous in the morning at my house.
And at the house of the absent child:

Hickory, dickory dock, the mice ran down the clock,
and the tears go by, this is the ending of the day
is done, gone the sun, and the swing low, sweet
cows lowing in the vega, he was twenty-three,
They're going to be crying a long time Amanda.

The sheeps in the meadow, the cows in the corn,
little Jack Horner come blow your
Taps, taps, for the children that fly away,
fly away, fly away home, cry wee wee wee
all the way,
where the heart is.

Getting to the heart of the matter
with Mary Jane, she's crying with all her might and Maine,
Remember the, Fire, fire,
Your nose is longer than a telephone wire,
Call the children, call the, X marks the spot,
where he happily ever after, and we all saw London Bridges
ashes, ashes, we all fall.

We called it macaroni, baby, baby,
close your eyes, go to sleep, may the angels watch
when the bough breaks the baby will fall,
cradle and
your house is on fire,
your children have flown, where
is the boy that looks after the sheep?

## DEARLY DEPARTED

Blessed is the darkness of the mother,
    that gave me the incendiary light.
The gift of language and laughter,
    and to know to put salt in the soup.
Blessed is the darkness of the mother.
    Her leaving me young, on the shores of my own future,
With my two babies and a yearning for poem.
Blessed is the darkness of the mother.
Let me borrow it for poems and lend it out again for prayers.
    For the men dying and dead of the virus in the night.
Blessed is the dark mother, for the best joke of the universe:
    not stand-up, but lay-down.
And her pretending to leave me here alone.
    As if any of us are really alone.
Blessed is the dark mother she had, she was
    I will become.

# A MOON CAN LOOK AT A POET

Everyone writes about Moons.
But moons are bored of us women,
Us leaky, lunar in our seasonal swing,
our wax and wane and silky pumps
that gleam moonshine on to dance floor and back again.
Click up your heels,
you slick mooned woman,
Ride a Cock Moon to Banbury bush.
Serve moons au gratin, moons and rice,
dip the moon lightly in wasabi and breathe fiery moon breathes.

For once, be moon. Moon all the way.
Say nothing you mean. Shift like sand.
Change daily.
Wear different bracelets every hour.
Look for silver in the cereal box.
Wear your beauty in quarter phases.
Buy three silk scarves.
Talk moonwise on a street corner,
and be in just enough danger.
Be heart pounding and dry mouthed alive in a crescent way.
Shine like the sun taught you,
backwards and back at the best man in the room.

Mugs of moon juice, lunar drafts, moon on tap,
lager moon, moon wine and gibbous tea.
The moon shining in day,
is tired of reading poems about herself by women,
and would rather dress in red and go to bars
or the Goddess Cafe for brunch.
She'll have huevos rancheros with green chile,
too many Bloody Marys,
and ride a palomino later if she's not too drunk.
Up into the cedar hills she'll go,
if a horse could carry a moon and he can,
and the moon wants to gallop her wild self
out of women's poems anyway.

## I BRAKE FOR ANGELS

My angel has work only I can do.
She told me last night,
as I drove, fast as ambition, to Santa Fe.
She pointed to a map of the world and said:
Move here.

I said, Where?
She said, here, you know, Earth.
Earth, New Mexico, I ask,
dodging a blue pick-up
that has changed lanes for the sole purpose of being in front of me.
No silly, Earth, Earth.
It's a deal, I say, When?

I am love, she says.

Uhh, are you still talking to me?
Rejoice in hope, she says.
Pardon, I ask.
A truck has passed me spewing rocks and grinding all gears.
Rejoice, she repeats loudly, in hope.
Is this still our conversation, I wonder,
and are you watching my windshield?

Love, she continues, is patient.
Patient, patient, I shriek.
The men on the road crew flag me down,
behind a line of cars too many to see past,
not enough to go yet.

Easy, she reminds me, does it.
Wait, come on, how do I know when I'm done,
when it's over?

I've been married thirteen years,
and it seems all I do is fix it, fix it, fix it,
like it, hate it, fix it. You get my drift.
My word, she says, is Truth.

Hey, I believe you, but I need a plan, a time frame.
I need a schedule, a phone number, 1-800-Rescue.
I need a way.

One day at a
Stop, I beg, I can't use this stuff.
It confuses me.
I just want an answer.

Turn, she says, left at the next right.

PEACE BUILDS STRONG BODIES 12 WAYS

When I heard America had declared war,
I thought, Oy, I better call Nancy.
What if the world ended & my sister and I still weren't speaking?

Bring the thoughts home.

Shop for peace. Peace lite, microwavable peace.
Peace in small cartons with straws to sip.
6 packs of peace and no preservatives added.

Charge and send peace on your Visa.
The 3rd World comes in every color.
Peace is so flattering, it looks good in teal, lavender & Kuwait.
Can you get the world economy in pink?

Peace is my color.
I look good in clean rivers and stands of pine.
I need fresh air to match.
Don't you?

Bring the thoughts home.

"They" didn't declare war.  Who were you angry at that day?
If you forgive your father, America won't need missiles.
Think global. Think positive.
What if they gave peace & everyone came?

It's exponential. It's mathematical.
Prayer x the width of the galaxy squared x Shabbos + candles
x the wingbeat of 1000 cranes =
The Gross National Product of Everywhere.

Bring the thoughts home.

My senator complains: You only call when you want something!
What a terrible houseguest!
Today I'll send lilacs and irises.
I'll write, Thank you for every vote that moves us towards life.

Bring the thoughts home.
Drink water. Take walks. Feed finches.
Wear scarves that float your beauty through air.
Accessorize your outfits with peace.
It's wash & wear. It's the latest.
One size fits all.

When someone wants war, we'll be too busy.
We're getting fuschia manicures, planting zinnas,
writing novels & french kissing.
We can't do war right now, we have to see the Monets.
We have to study Chinese, learn astronomy, take up belly dancing.

We're on Hyde Mountain watching Zonetails,
at the movies, crying our eyes out.
We're in bed with each other and good coffee.
We're playing alto sax and eating spinach salad.
We're busy sending our compliments to the chef & lingering over dessert.
We're eating more chocolate & winning at team sports.

Bring the thoughts home.

There are children in the Mid-East who sleep to sirens.
Don't we owe them a lullabye?
There are children in your town whose parents hurt them.
Wouldn't you tuck them in at night if you could?
And did you praise your children & your Nana & your lover today?
And what about wind power anyway?

Pain in the energy?
Take 2 solars and call me in the morning.
Heat your house with active peace.
I don't know from oil, but I know what I like.

Peace is high protein.
Peace is slenderizing. It's low fat and good for the heart.
It's analgesic.
It's antiseptic.
It's organic and completely recylable.
Peace is a renewable resource.
It's a pyschic phenomenon.
It's aerobic.
Just do it.

# DON'T SHOW THIS TO ANYONE

This poem is respectfully dedicated to Larry Hill,

April 4th, 1952 - October 8th, 1990

We say it quietly,
he's sick, he may not be here next year,
he can't do that, he's not well enough.
AIDS is his secret, his Buddha, his honey,
his lunch he eats alone in covetous silence every day.
He's alone a lot, cleans the house, takes naps.
His death is our secret.
We say, are you up to that? He isn't.
We tiptoe. We whisper.
Death is the biggest secret.
Sotto voce, we say, He's sick,
we say, This could be the last time,
we say, Don't overdo, How are you, How was your day
and we mean, you made it another day.
His thinness and pallor, blue lips.
What can we do? His death is no secret.
He's sick and we know and he knows.
At dinner I notice him white and shaking.
He needs to leave. Is it secret?
He's not telling but we leave.
AIDS, AIDS is the secret of the century.
He has AIDS has AIDS has AIDS.
I've said it now. He's dying.
He's here to say good-bye to us.
This is the last visit, the last talk,
the last drive to Chimayo for apple margaritas,
for holy dirt that can't cure the biggest secret,
that can't stop the wind whistling through every
conversation
and the lightning on the horizon
saying last, last, and never.
We can't fix him, like a rotor,
or the muffler on the car, or the baby's tricycle
or my new beaded earrings.
Take a thousand vitamins, and do color meditation,
Wish on stars. Don't keep it secret,
maybe it will come true.

## DRESSED FOR WINTER

This is how you can walk safely
over the soft places.
As if it were raining in a foreign country.
As if the sky was learning a certain shade of green from the lake.
While the black bear asleep in his January cave
dreams of moss and red berries come ripe.
It's that easy.
You can swim over the soft places, humming quietly.
Something you've forgotten the words to,
Something you never knew,
but found, in the torn out pocket of your thick coat.

# A WIND BY ANY OTHER NAME

I know this wind.
This wind took my life, blew my children to the Holy Land.
All that's left is their pictures, outgrown clothes and crib toys.
I come home and my desk is rearranged.
I find poems by Beaudelaire on the floor,
the Marquis de Sade's leathers in the bathrooms.
My father's razor in my shoe.

My grandmother's teeth have blown in and hang from a lace shawl
that may have belonged to Marie Antoinette.
France has blown in and the whole Cubist period.
Bracque's in the kitchen putting his whole heart into the bouillabaise.
The Blue Guitar, missing a string,
is on my mother's yellow chinoiserie sofa in a new room
the wind has added on to the house.
·
It's a dojo, and 20 students blow in doing T'ai chi
and experiencing their haras.
I can't experience mine.
The wind has taken it & blown to Kabal,
where it's joined the Mujahedim, and they're taking Afganistan back.

Revolutions blow in and new planets.
The universe is practicing the Chaos Theory.
The cosmos is writing on turbulence for 10 timed minutes:
Not mentioning fractals, not saying riverbed,
Not describing fluid dynamics, just raising white water,
and swelling the Rio up to the sandstone banks.


There's no rhyme or reason,
only sand in my teeth, and Keat's blowing by on a white horse,
worrying about negative capability and drinking absinthe.

45

It's the witch peddling past Dorothy, and the music goes:
da da da da da tah, da da da da da tah.
But this is Kansas and the women run amuck with axes,
take the house back down, rip the sheets off the line,
pack the Conestoga up,
and head east or west or anywhere the crazy wind isn't.

Snow blows in, other seasons and my childhood.
I'm 12 and my boyfriend is going to leave me for Nancy Troy.
I'm in the girl's bathroom rolling up my skirt and having a cig.
Annie B. whirls in and the whole Civil War and Chem 2.
And I'm doing well, because the answers to everything have arrived.
A sudden gust, dust devil & I'm going gangbuster's in Latin.
I love Virgil and dactyllic hexameter.

Armo virumque cano blows in
and a slice with extra cheese from the Havapizza on 86th.
Lexington Avenue is there and Bloomingdales.
I'm trying on man-tailored shirts, Villager skirts
and worrying about Viet Nam.
Ho Chi Minh and Chairman Mao ride the 96th street crosstown home with me
but New York blows away and I'm older and have two kids
and dogs and cats and birds and a husband
and a regular life with Tuesdays and doctor appointments
and clearing the table.

Now what I have is whirling too fast to name.
I'm not even sure it's mine. It could be yours.
In this weather there's no way to tell.

## WOMEN AND DEATH

We die into a 1000 bouquets of red roses,
wrapped in old copies of Vogue and Paris Match.
We die into the Venus of Willendorf,
all belly and curve.
We die into the caves in Lascaux.
We were bison and the Sybil's words.
Rattling the shin bone of deer and mountain goat.

We die into Eurynome, dancing the great wind of creation
into darkness, sky, light and sea.
We die into Crete and Naxos,
Ariadne left alone, marrying the wine god, in madness,
griefswept.

We die into Lilith, and Susannah.
into Deborah, woman of light,
into Ameratsu, Kali, Tiamat, Yemaya
Kuan Yin,
mother of day, mother of night.

We die into Sicilian Nonas
dressed in black, opening the door,
offering bowls of plums and cherries,
all manner of fruit with inner stones.

We die into triangle and circle,
I counted every degree, came up equilateral,
arrows pointing South.
There was a faceted bottle of scent.
The instructions, as always, read: Drink me.

I drink it. One exact ounce and tasted
bergamot, ambergris and jaguar.
I died for real then, into a landscape of frozen light.
I heard the sound of the ice crust breaking:
Air coming up for air.

I died with twelve women, all slowly pulling their clothes off.
Saying to their bodies,
There, now, there.
I planted the roses in that place,
And they bloomed, they bloomed.

## A WOMAN PRACTICES CHAOS THEORY

I am becoming a woman of alfalfa and silence.
I am becoming a woman of walks, walks in wind,
the beat of air against my own heart.
I am a river of silence, but full of stories of Descartes.
In this story, he sits, not on a bench, but on a bus.
He computes existence in terms of travel,
decides that rest stops and ice tea are infinite.
He drinks therefore he is.
He measures time in red points on the map.
6, 12, 15 miles between dots.
He hopes it's real.

I am real.
I've never been so real, and I know this because when I wait,
my heart ticks as loudly as wind through the Pinon on my road.
I want to rest then, close my eyes, and just hold
on the hillside where Yucca blooms have gone to worried seed,
the last fuschia moments of Cholla.

I am a woman of belief and stone.
Marble lives, not in museums,
but on my steps, waiting for thrust and grind.
I wait for thrust and grind also,
but I am becoming a woman of patience.
I imagine loving Van Gogh, waiting for sunflowers, cypress
& starry skies to be poured onto canvas in windy rushes,
while I lie in bed in a fever of breeze and desire.

Imagine Seurat's lover,
waiting for the park to emerge from a field of dots.
When he stretched that huge canvas,
She must have heard the sound of water lapping,
lapping against her life,

and wine, wine swirling in a glass.

It's a resonant frequency. The world curling out and out.
Waiting for the next thought, the next sweeping curve.

I am a woman with a mission of wind.
I sweep through words, through the exact flowers
that bloom in late July.
Orange Mallow and the purple Spiderwort.
My days smell sweet to me,
walking through words, winds and fields,
waiting for the sheen on cherrywood,
watching clouds practice being less.

I am becoming diffuse as these delicate patterns,
an emergent form,
fractal woman of my own making.

# ANGELS PART THE CLOUDS

A woman runs in pines, in snow.
breath catching in her throat.
It's cold, cold
and clouds part at her feet, suddenly eye level.
She's running.
Running from the business of business, from loss
from checkbooks, a balance of loss, anxious deposits,
and withdrawals of lack.

She's lacking.
She's lacking in time, lacking in money
and worse, no jokes for this.
She's running in steamy puffs of visible air
and doesn't know how much poverty it takes
to screw in a light bulb.

She's praying.
She's thanking God for this road where this summer
she saw four deer, and now,
there is always the possibility of deer,
forever a chance to know swift flight and soft fur
slipping over hills.
She's praying, running and praising, Modah Ani.

She's grateful.
Grateful for the wind that plays the boughs,
a Corelli of winter, a Bach of lifting and moving on.
She's running.
Running in a world that's white,
that starts over daily
without the carried negative balance,
without the fear in the mailbox,
without the lack.

She's running.
Her thighs ache in the stretch and contract,
blood pulsing, and she's grateful
and lacking
and running
and praying
in cold snow and the chance of seeing deer disappear into forest.

# LUMINOUS STAR FINDER

Stars kindle loneliness into absolute magnitude,
entwined in my daughter's once-long hair.
We are drowning in the mother-daughter darkness.
Comets catapult out and away,
beyond Mercury and language.

We find each other lit by the eyes that watch all night.
I watch her sleep.
Blink and see her jitterbugging across the moon.
It's a skyscape of family,
full of hidden galaxies and half-finished sentences.

Punctuation floats over us like a meteor shower.
Every conversation is a black hole,
even Stephen Hawking doesn't understand.
Hello, hello hello, I shout. Anyone out there?
There, comes the echo, rebounding through nebulae.

It's planetary.
Love without gravity or mass.
On earth, apples float up, endlessly up.
You couldn't hold them if you tried.

New constellations appear in the autumn sky.
Star clouds glitter in Cygnus, the Swan.
Binary pairs held by a common center,
orchards of light.

## I THINK I HAVE ALWAYS SEEN

A mulberry is not a drum, and does not long to be.
I learn quiet from the leave's rustle.
Stillness from the root's way of holding tight in red dirt.
A tree is the same alive as poem.

Ophelia did not hang herself from an oak,
but laid under its broad and brooding shadows in a river.
She cannot live, Shakespeare says,
because she is a woman "incapable of her own sorrow".
If Ophelia had known to climb trees, Hamlet would have married her.

The birch tree loves me. He told me so.
He said, Make your desk from my clear, light wood
and your words will ring with truth.
I love him back, have tucked a note in his criss-cross bark.
Be with me always, I write.
A sentiment a tree can understand.

Willows sing in wind, in their own scale.
Jazz trees thrumming to the beat of the blow.
Willows wail & whip, throw their thick green hair back
like Billie, like Bessie.
Willows have enough grief to do blues serious.
An impulse towards tears swings in their veins.

The juniper is hunched, howling witch woman on the hillside.
This is why the jays do not touch her berries.

The cherry's heart is a mantra. I know it too.
Have always.
By night, I am also root, bark
and whatever is reaching out in air.

Sigmund has an elm on the couch.
Carl has a chestnut in the waiting room, writing down dreams.
The elm hates his father, and the chestnut,
has of course, dreamt a mandala.

Tree x tree = forest.
An equation beloved to trees includes much carbon dioxide,
which they willingly convert to oxygen.
In other times, humans worshipped them for this.

Spring, we smell the heat around the locust,
as they blossom into crimson.
The cottonwood woos us with billowing drift.
There is no end to the luminous performance of trees.

The pinon is my way of knowing home.
As aspens flicker, so do I.
You are not only my sunshine,
I tell my lover, but my mahogany, my peach, my alder.
I turn in your hands, as on a lathe of desire.

When the leaves blow inside out,
I know it will rain.

Chaplin walks happy down a depression street.
He has talked for the first time.
He and Paulette Godard are in love with each other & the future.
The future is known to the eucalyptus & sycamores.
And that is how it has always been.

## SAMURAI ANGELS

I heard your name in my dream last night.
It was your childhood name and I was calling you.
There was an angel on every stair.
There was light from four directions.

It was your childhood name and I was calling you.
Tell me eleven names for wind, I said.
There was light from four directions.
Tell me how you followed the scent of daffodils
through the streets of London.

Tell me eleven names for wind, I said.
I'm one thought away.
Tell me how you found a square filled with flowers
in a dark city.
The angels are calling our names out loud.

I'm one landscape away.
Any moment could be Japan.
The angels are calling our names out loud.
Their wings are light and cherry blossom, we could hear
temple bells ringing on any street.

Any landscape could be Japan.
You were born there.
There will always be plum blossoms, can't you hear the silence
in the temples around us?
I can write you three lines and there will be cranes in all of them.

You were born there.
After love we breathe in Japanese,
our sleeping bodies form the character for light.
I can write you three lines and there will be the way you loved
your father in all of them.
There's a secret in Haiku: I'll tell you.

After love we breathe in Japanese, our sleeping bodies
form the character for angel.
After love the taste of saki is silky and fierce.
There's a secret, I'll tell you:
Haiku is really four lines, but the last line is silent.

After love the taste of saki is silky and fierce.
See how gently I write us into your past.
The fourth line in Haiku is a temple.
I call your secret name for the last time.

See how delicately I write us into your past.
Under Fujiyama, I know you are weeping.
I call your childhood name for the last time.
I hold you. Your tears rhyme with the grain of light woods,
The sound of taps for your father.

# GRIST FOR GRACE

Let me speak for the gray-green lichen,
Know how the Blackjacks go crone in harsh weather,
or on account of mistletoe.
Help me say how winter comes in on a red-gold downbeat,
an orchestra of oak.

Sing me a forest.
Sing me in the sweet pitch of ochre, the bassy rusts.
Play me in the key of mountains,
Rising always above myself.
Hum the rustling needles of the pine's constant undressing.
Make me naked to any season.

Make me open to the tender rays of late sun.
Call my name in the sounds of absent water.
Write my address this way:
Turn right at the quartzite boulder,
go straight 'til you remember your first kiss
and the smell of toast that first morning.

Dress me in evergreen, in blue spruce and fir.
Make an altar of the ordinary.
Pinon cones and the feathers of Steller jays.
Write me a simple story, hummingbird's soar,
raven's wing and rock bed.

Tickle me with turkey feathers.
Make me laugh.
How many religions does it take to screw in a light bulb ?
Dance me along a sacred maze, back into my body,
That other, most hallowed ground.

## GRANTED

Grant me the ability to be alone.
Grant me the gift of gab, the jabber of jays.
Grant me the wide, lyrical view:
The way the Red-Tail knows the world to be.

Grant me a perch on the fine edge of fences.
Make me fly up startled, like the swallows at evening time.
Gather me into the tight V of snow geese,
Flying across the Bosque moon.

Call me in the huzzahs of wind,
Sing to me in the timbres of horizon.
Show me the distance plotted by rivers.
Make it rain, but just lightly.
The warm world wash that brings up the wild blue iris, the beebalm.

Re-seed,me.
Scatter me north, that I might glitter in the dusk like snowfall.
Scatter me east, that I might rise glamorous in my own morning.
Scatter me south, that I may blow sultry back into your day,
Be an island of palms and peace.
Scatter me west that I may set in your heart and rest there.

## ABSOLUTELY X

When I carve a hyperbolic curve, you tell me,
and enter those relations,
I am in alignment with God.
When you tell me of hyperbolic curves,
I'm in alignment with God!
I love it when you talk dirty:
Tell me about the laws of physical matter
present in the hulls of ships,
and I'm on fire.
Tell me the divine nature of curved form
is always speaking to us about Creation,
and I'm weak in the knees.
Every thought is a kind of ecstatic stroking, and I come home,
to the sounding presence of my womanself in your words.
Carve me a hull!
Tell me about mortise and tenons.
Show me the perfect line in that sweet tongue and groove.
I'm longing for wood and measure,
held in the bench vise of desire.
Speak to me in sculpture,
Teach me the articulate gesture of design.
Use words like grain and tensile,
and I'm turning too, becoming a new shape.
Shape of a woman inflamed with the need for oak,
in heat for birch.
Say the names of trees and I am coming
more and more home to this world,
where the sawdust lays at our feet,
and we're ready to dive in,
to that place where the material has dissolved.

# THE LAST STORY

For Dolores LaChapelle

Tell it in Denaina, let the clicked
syllabic beat break ice.
Drop down into blackberry narrative.
Shift the space key.
It's Alaska, Alaska and compression into shale,
seven species of swallow.
Be pushed into stillness. It's calm here.
Nothing shifts underfoot.
We know where we stand and responsibility lies.
We look ourselves up in poems.
We are filed into stanza,
made into 14 lines, become sonnet,
end in couplet.

Make a relation. Get lexical.
It's research.
Our text is basin, is Big Bear creek,
is Cook Inlet.
New York City appears, and the high rises
fold in on themselves.
Become the Hudson River valley and we stretch
from Mancos to Inuit to Silverpick.

We are elastic. A yoga of lyric.
Ochre, we say.
Naming a color and hoping we've dug to root.
The land speaks to us.
A transliteration of heave, swell and shifting plates.
Slow salt water syllables wash over,
and we become fluid.
It's news and you've come here to say it
in a dialect of clang and watershed.

Suddenly, we leap lattices.
Open a dictionary,
All the meanings shift down one entry.
Every word means the next thought.
Takes us the deepest place we know,
Beneath Venus rising and Jupiter setting.
Beneath pond ice and under algae.


Travel to the source.
Get interested. Drop down into consonants.
Let the vowels out to play.
A is on the swing. Ahhhhh,
we go up, rise into ptarmigan call,
the haunting cry of loon.
See the Red-Tail's view of Shandokah
curling up and up from below.
Eeee, we say. Knees pull back down and in.
Pump. Sing the see-saw song.
Marjorie Daw.
Jack shall have a new master.
One of his own choice.
He shall have but a penny a day
Let's go faster.


Remember, the secret Torah is not written.
One day we'll open the scrolls
Find the letters have skipped, skipped
skipped to My Lou.
Sand cranes will appear,
telling their name in Navajo, Farsi,
mysterious polyphonic tongues we don't know yet.
Can't know, so mutter them,
gutteral, swallow.
Talk in cluck and gasp.
Breathe hard, make a sound
like rain, pour down consonants, P, D, T, K
and B. Not soothing -